South West Coast Path

Dorset

■ This publication covers the Dorset section of the South West Coast Path, a National Trail extending 630 miles from Minehead in Somerset to Poole Harbour in Dorset and including a great variety of landscape, wildlife and geology.

■ Containing Ordnance Survey 'Explorer' maps in a convenient book format with an index to the main features, each of the five books show all footpaths, rights of way and public access land, and are the essential companion whether tackling the entire route or enjoying a relaxing afternoon walk along the famous Dorset Jurassic Coast.

CONTENTS

A-Z Az AtoZ
registered trade marks of
Geographers' A-Z Map Company Ltd

www./az.co.uk

EDITION 2 2015
Copyright © Geographers' A-Z Map Company Ltd.
Telephone: 01732 781000 (Enquiries & Trade Sales)
01732 783422 (Retail Sales)

© Crown copyright and database rights 2015. OS 100017302.

1:25 000 'Explorer' maps are sourced from Ordnance Survey.
Public rights of way shown on these maps have been taken from local authority definitive maps and later amendments.
The representation on the maps of any other road, track or footpath is no evidence of the existence of a right of way.

© Natural England (2014) material is reproduced with the permission of Natural England, http://www.naturalengland.org.uk/copyright

Communications

ROADS AND PATHS

Not necessarily rights of way

 Service Areas

 Junction number

M I or A 6(M) — Motorway

A 35 — Dual carriageway

A 30 — Main road

B 3074 — Secondary road

Narrow road with passing places

Road under construction

Road generally more than 4m wide

Road generally less than 4m wide

Other road, drive or track, fenced and unfenced

>> > Gradient: steeper than 20% (1 in 5); 14% (1 in 7) to 20% (1 in 5)

Ferry — Ferry; Ferry P – passenger only

Path

RAILWAYS

Multiple track standard gauge

Single track standard gauge

Narrow gauge or Light rapid transit system (LRTS) and station

Road over; road under; level crossing

Cutting; tunnel; embankment

Station, open to passengers; siding

PUBLIC RIGHTS OF WAY

(Rights of way are not shown on maps of Scotland)

----------- Footpath — — — — Bridleway

++++++ Byway open to all traffic

Restricted byway (not for use by mechanically propelled vehicles)

Public rights of way shown on this map have been taken from local authority definitive maps and later amendments. Rights of way are liable to change and may not be clearly defined on the ground. Please check with the relevant local authority for the latest information.

The representation on this map of any other road, track or path is no evidence of the existence of a right of way.

OTHER PUBLIC ACCESS

• • • Other routes with public access (not normally shown in urban areas)

The exact nature of the rights on these routes and the existence of any restrictions may be checked with the local highway authority. Alignments are based on the best information available.

◆ ◆ ⬤ National Trail
◯ One mile distance marker

 South West Coast Path

◆ ◇ ◆ Recreational Route

◇ ◇ Alternative (England Coast path only)

--------- Permissive footpath

— — — Permissive bridleway

Footpaths and bridleways along which landowners have permitted public use but which are not rights of way. The agreement may be withdrawn.

 Traffic-free cycle route

1 National cycle network route number – traffic free

1 National cycle network route number – on road

 Firing and test ranges in the area. Danger! Observe warning notices

Visit www.access.mod.uk for information

ACCESS LAND   England

Access land portrayed on this map is intended as a guide to land normally available for access on foot, for example access land created under the Countryside and Rights of Way Act 2000, and land managed by the National Trust, Forestry Commission and Woodland Trust. Some restrictions will apply; some land shown as access land may not have open land access rights; always refer to local signage.

⬠ Access land

▨ Access land in woodland area

ℹ Access information point

🌀🌀🌀 Coastal Margin — All land within the 'coastal margin' is associated with the England Coast Path. Visit: www.nationaltrail.co.uk/england-coast-path

The depiction of rights of access does not imply or express any warranty as to its accuracy or completeness. Observe local signs and follow the Countryside Code. Visit www.naturalengland.org.uk

 Access permitted within managed controls for example, local bylaws Visit www.access.mod.uk

General Information

BOUNDARIES

— — + — — + — National

— · — · — · — County (England)

— — — — — Unitary Authority (UA), Metropolitan District (Met Dist), London Borough (LB) or District (Scotland & Wales are solely Unitary Authorities)

· · · · · · · · · Civil Parish (CP) (England) or Community (C) (Wales)

━━ ━━ National Park boundary

VEGETATION

Limits of vegetation are defined by positioning of symbols

Coniferous trees

Non-coniferous trees

Coppice

Bracken, heath or rough grassland

Marsh, reeds or saltings

Orchard

Scrub

GENERAL FEATURES

+	Place of worship	△ Ⱦ	Triangulation pillar; mast	BP/BS — Boundary post/stone
	Current or former place of worship	⚒	Windmill, with or without sails	CG — Cattle grid
⚲	with tower			CH — Clubhouse
⚲	with spire, minaret or dome	Ⱦ Ⱦ	Wind pump; wind turbine	FB — Footbridge
☐ ☐	Building; important building	pylon pole	Electricity transmission line	MP ; MS — Milepost; milestone
▨	Glasshouse	⊓⊓⊓⊓⊓⊓	Slopes	Mon — Monument
▲	Youth hostel			PO — Post office
■	Bunkhouse/camping barn/other hostel			Pol Sta — Police station
⬗	Bus or coach station			Sch — School
🗼 🗼 🗼	Lighthouse; disused lighthouse; beacon			TH — Town hall
				NTL — Normal tidal limit
				W; Spr — Well; spring

Gravel pit   Sand pit

Other pit or quarry   Landfill site or slag/spoil heap

HEIGHTS AND NATURAL FEATURES

52 · Ground survey height

284 · Air survey height

Surface heights are to the nearest metre above mean sea level. Where two heights are shown, the first is the height of the natural ground at the triangulation pillar and the second (in brackets) is to the highest natural summit.

Vertical face/cliff

Loose rock   Boulders   Outcrop   Scree

75
60
50

Contours may be at 5 or 10 metres vertical interval

☐ Water

▨ Mud

☐ Sand; sand & shingle

ARCHAEOLOGICAL AND HISTORICAL INFORMATION

⚒	Site of antiquity	✲ ⊓⊓⊓	Visible earthwork
⚔ 1066	Site of battle (with date)	VILLA	Roman
		Castle	Non-Roman

Information provided by English Heritage for England and the Royal Commissions on the Ancient and Historical Monuments for Scotland and Wales

Selected Tourist and Leisure Information

P Parking	⛺ Camp site	🚲 Cycle hire	🐋 Fishing
P&R Park & Ride, - all year	🚐 Caravan site	⋃ Horse riding	☆ Other tourist feature
P&R - seasonal	🏃 Recreation leisure sports centre	⚡ Viewpoint	✝ Cathedral/Abbey
i Information cen. - all year	⚑ Golf course or links	✕ Picnic site	🏛 Museum
i - seasonal	♨ Theme pleasure park	👁 Country park	🏰 Castle/fort
V Visitor centre	🚂 Preserved railway	❀ Garden arboretum	🏛 Building of historic interest
Forestry Commission visitor centre	☕ Public house/s	⛵ Water activities	🏛 Heritage centre
PC Public convenience	⚒ Craft centre	⛵ Slipway	▩ National Trust
☎ Telephone - public	❗ Walks/trails	⛵ Boat trips	▦ English Heritage
☎ - roadside assistance	🚲 Cycle trail	⛵ Boat hire	◈ World Heritage site/area
☎ - emergency	🚵 Mountain bike trail	🦆 Nature reserve	

1 Kilometre = 0.6214 mile
1 metre = 3.2808 feet

Scale 1:25 000

1 mile = 1.6093 kilometres
100 feet = 30.48 metres

1000 m   0   1 km

3000 feet   0   1/2 mile

KEY TO MAP PAGES

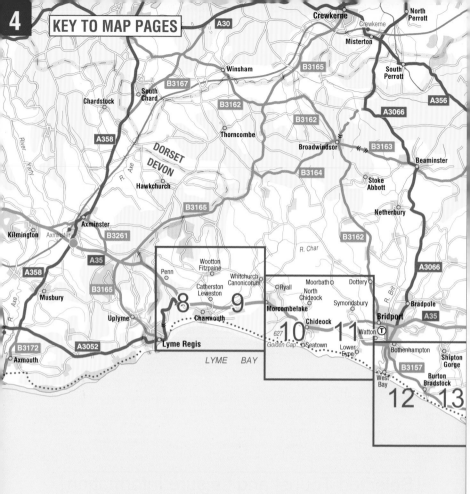

Crewkerne
North Perrott
Crewkerne
Misterton
South Perrott
A30
A356
Winsham
B3165
B3167
South Chard
B3162
B3162
A3066
Chardstock
B3163
A358
Thorncombe
Broadwindsor
Beaminster
DORSET
DEVON
B3164
Stoke Abbott
Hawkchurch
Netherbury
R. Axe
B3165
B3162
Axminster
A3066
Kilmington
B3261
Axminster
R. Char
A35
Bradpole
A358
Wootton Fitzpaine
Penn
Moorbath
Dottery
Bridport
Musbury
B3165
Catherston
Leweston
Whitchurch
Canonicorum
Ryall
North
Chideock
Symondsbury
A35
Watton
R. Brit
Uplyme
8
9
Morcombelake
11
Charmouth
Chideock
Bothenhampton
Shipton Gorge
B3172
A3052
Lyme Regis
627
10
Golden Cap
Seatown
Lower Eype
West Bay
B3157
Burton Bradstock
Axmouth
R. Axe
LYME   BAY
12
13

E N G L I S H

SCALE (1:200,000)

0   1   2   3   4   5 Miles

0 1 2 3 4   5 Kilometres

South West Coast Path • • • • • • • • •

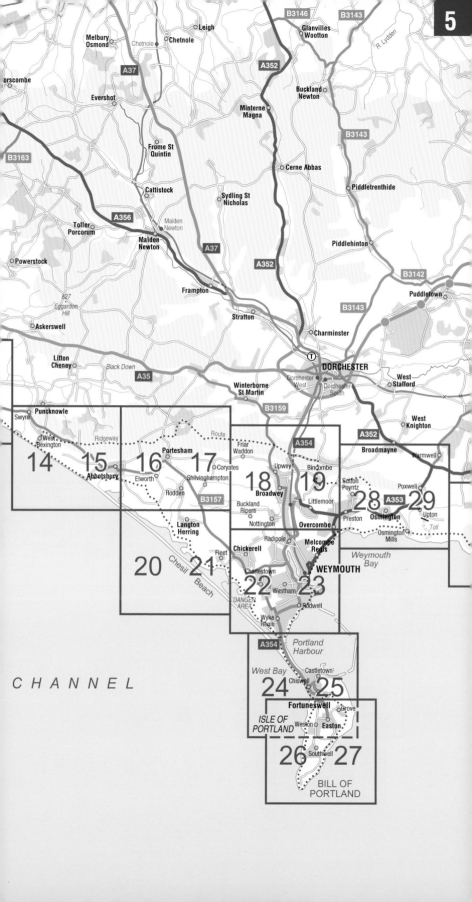

KEY TO MAP PAGES

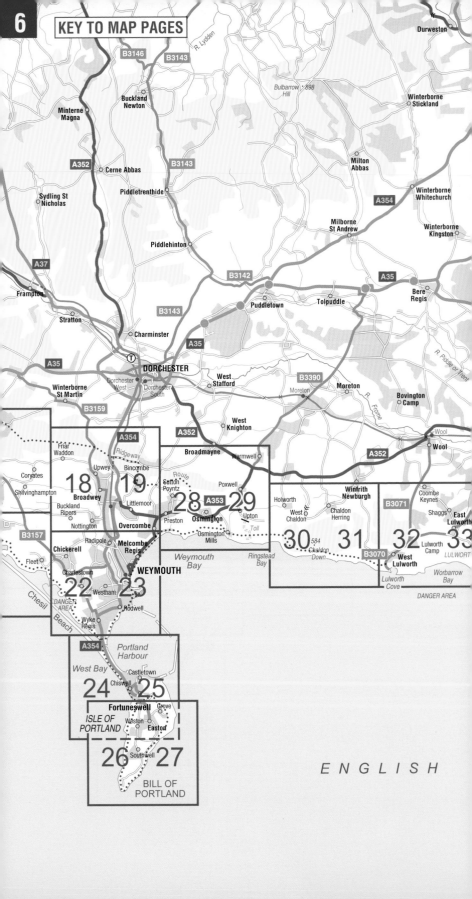

Durweston

B3146
B3143
R. Lydden
Bulbarrow · 898 Hill
Winterborne Stickland

Buckland Newton
Minterne Magna
Milton Abbas

A352
Cerne Abbas
B3143
Winterborne Whitechurch
A354

Sydling St Nicholas
Piddletrenthide
Milborne St Andrew
Winterborne Kingston

A37
Piddlehinton
B3142
Frampton
B3143
Puddletown
Tolpuddle
A35
Bere Regis

Stratton
Charminster
A35
R. Piddle or Trent

A35
DORCHESTER
T
Dorchester West
West Stafford
B3390
Moreton
R. Frome
Wool

Winterborne St Martin
Dorchester South
West Knighton
Moreton
Bovington Camp
Wool

B3159
A354
A352
Wool

Friar Waddon
Ridgeway
Broadmayne
Warmwell
A352

Coryates
Upwey
Bincombe
Winfrith Newburgh
B3071
Coombe Keynes

Shilvinghampton
18 Broadwey
19
Sutton Poyntz
Poxwell
Holworth
West Chaldon
Chaldon Herring
Shaggs
East Lulworth

Buckland Ripers
Littlemoor
28 A353 **29** Upton Toll
30 584 Chaldon Down
31
32 Lulworth Camp
33 LULWORTH

Nottington
Overcombe
Preston
Osmington
Osmington Mills
Ringstead Bay
B3070
West Lulworth
Worbarrow Bay

B3157
Radipole
Melcombe Regis
Weymouth Bay
Lulworth Cove
Chickerell
22 **23** WEYMOUTH
DANGER AREA

Fleet
Charlestown
Westham
DANGER AREA

Chesil Beach
Rodwell

Wyke Regis

A354
Portland Harbour
West Bay
Castletown

24 Chiswell **25**

ISLE OF PORTLAND
Fortuneswell
Grove
Weston
Easton

26 Southwell **27**

BILL OF PORTLAND

E N G L I S H

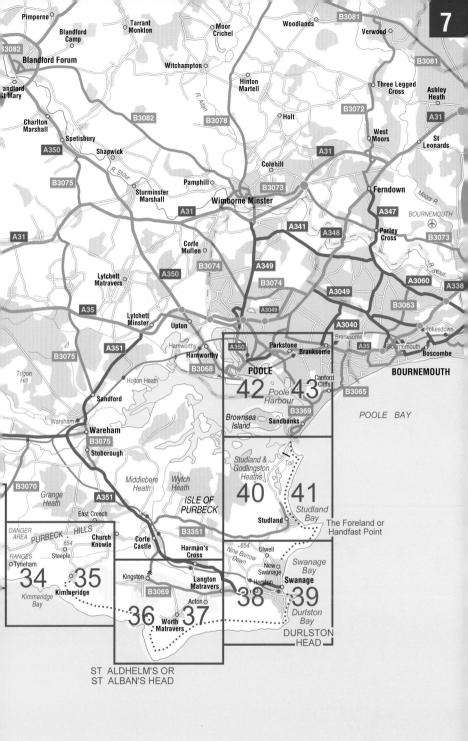

Pimperne
Tarrant Monkton
Moor Crichel
Woodlands
B3081
Verwood

Blandford Camp
B3082
Blandford Forum
Witchampton
Three Legged Cross
Ashley Heath
B3081

andford St Mary
Hinton Martell
A31

Charlton Marshall
B3082
B3078
Holt
B3072
West Moors
St Leonards

Spetisbury
A350
Colehill
Ferndown
Moors R.

Shapwick
R. Stour
Pamphill
B3073
BOURNEMOUTH
A347
Parley Cross
B3073

B3075
Sturminster Marshall
A31
Wimborne Minster
A31
A341
A348

A31
Corfe Mullen
A350
B3074
A349
B3074
A3049
A3060
A338
B3063

Lytchett Matravers
A35
A3049
A3040
A3049
Branksome
A35
Pokesdown
Boscombe

Lytchett Minster
Upton
Hamworthy
A350
Parkstone
Branksome
Bournemouth
BOURNEMOUTH

B3075
Holton Heath
Hamworthy
B3068
POOLE
42 43
Canford Cliffs
B3065

Trigon Hill
Sandford
Poole Harbour
B3369
POOLE BAY

Wareham
Brownsea Island
Sandbanks

B3075
Stoborough
Studland & Godlingston Heaths
40 41
Studland Bay

B3070
Grange Heath
A351
Middlebere Heath
Wytch Heath
ISLE OF PURBECK
Studland
The Foreland or Handfast Point

East Creech
PURBECK HILLS
Church Knowle
Corfe Castle
B3351
Harman's Cross
Nine Barrow Down
·654
Ulwell
New Swanage
Swanage Bay

DANGER AREA
654
Steeple
Kingston
Langton Matravers
Herston
Swanage
38 39

RANGES
Tyneham
34 35
Kimmeridge
B3069
Acton
Worth Matravers
36 37
Durlston Bay

Kimmeridge Bay

ST ALDHELM'S OR ST ALBAN'S HEAD
DURLSTON HEAD

C H A N N E L

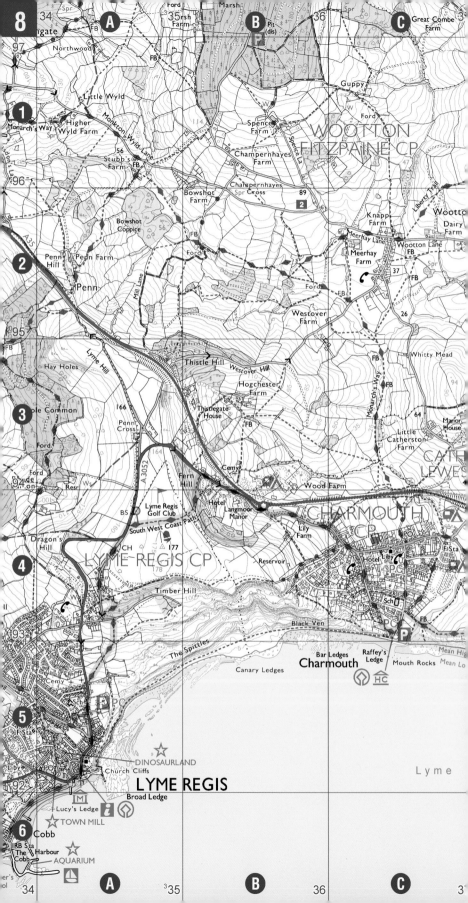

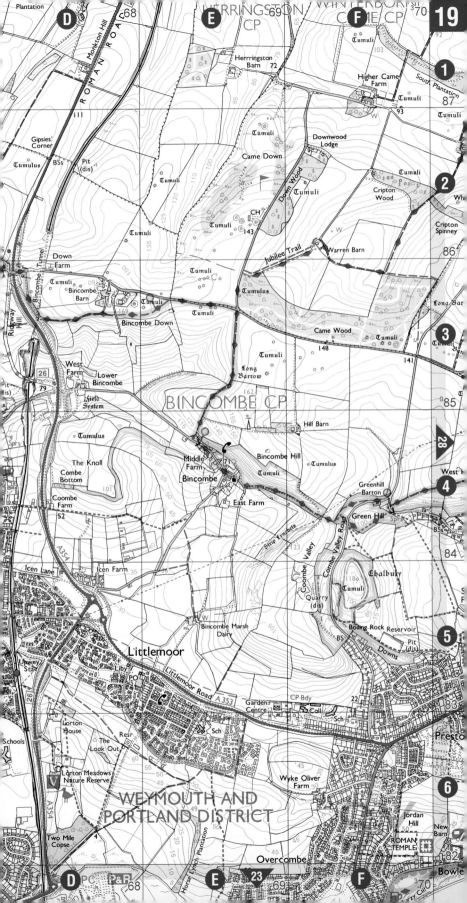

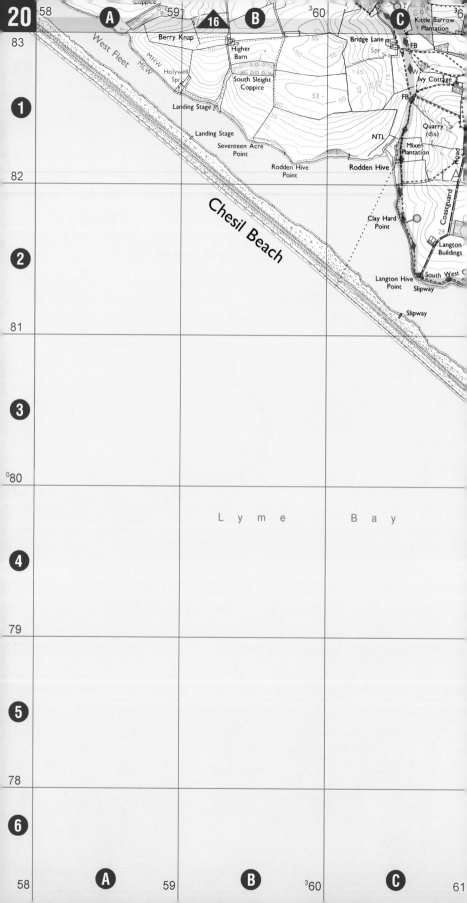

A 22 B C

1

76

2

⁰75

3

74

4

73

5

72

6

71

³65 A 66 B 67 C 68

Chesil Beach Holiday Village

Jetty

Small Mouth

Ferry Bridge

Rifle Range (disused)

Portland Coast Path 3

Dismantled Railway

V PC

P

England Coast Path

National Sailing Academy

South West Coast Path

West Bay

26

Tar Rocks

Clay C

Blacknor

Mutton Cove

Tar Rocks
Clay Ope

West Weare
West Cliff

Tout
Quarry
Sculpture
Park

Inmosthay
Quarries

f13

Wks

Qua
(dis)

Bowers
Quarries

Cemy

Coll

Blacknor

Mutton Cove

Weston

Lawr

PO

67

Quarry
(dis)

68

Southwell

Combefield
Quarries

Lawnsheds

Sch

68

Sweet Hill

Portland Coast Path

59

S.W.C. Path

Sand

Wallsend Cove

Field System

Lawnsheds

Culver Well

28

Quarries
(dis)

54

Lawnsheds

FB

Lookout
Station

Cave Hole

Lloyds
Cottage

Bird
Observatory

Cave

Blow Hole

Rocket Post

P

Cave

White Hole
Pulpit Rock

PO

V

Obelisk

Portland Bill

South West
Coast Path
73

King Barrow
Quarries
(dis)

Admiralty
Quarries

Folly Pier

1

72

PORTLAND

Wks

Sch

Independant
Quarries

HM
Young Offender
Institution

A 354

Grove

F Sta

P

Broadcroft Quarry
Butterfly Reserve

Easton

Yeolands
Quarry

Durdle Pier

2

71

Quarries
(dis)

Bottom
Coombe

Penn's
Weare

Portland

heds

Perryfield
Quarries

Rufus Castle
(rems of)
church
(rems of)

Church Ope
Cove

Quarry
(dis)

Southwell Landslip

Freshwater Bay

3

⁰70

P.C Path St

Quarries
(dis)

Quarries
(dis)
God Nore

4

mekiln Cave
oles

69

E n g l i s h   *C h a n n e l*

5

68

SY

6

34

88 · 89 · 90 · 91

Tumulus
East Holme Range · A · Clay Pit West Creech · B · Tumulus · Mine (dis) · C
West Creech Farm · Little Wood
Creech

1
Tumulus
Povington
Povington Wood
82 Povington Barrow
Ws · Spr

DANGER AREA MOD RANGES OBSERVE WARNING NOTICES TYNEHAM CP

2
Quarry (dis)
Pit (dis) · 168
Pump House (dis) · 173
STEEPLE CP · P
West Creech Hill
Quarry (dis) · 174
Quarry (dis)
Povington Hill · 187
Quarry (dis)
Lutton Gwyle
84 · 73 · Pur
Manor Far
81 Quarry (dis)
Pit (dis)
Lutton

33
94
Rook Grove
North Egliston
109
Chapel Close · Earthworks
Steeple Leaze Farm · 83

3
Tyneham
Earthworks
68
Tyneham Farm · Tyneham House (remains of) · Tyneham Great Wood
P
80
Shepherd's Cottage

Pit (dis)
South Egliston (ruins)
Tyneham Cap · Spr
Egliston Gwyle
Higher Stonehips

4
134
Gad Cliff · MLW
75 · Lower Stonehips
Wagon Rock
Brandy Bay · 35 · Oil Well
Gaulte Gap

79
Long Ebb · 20 · 17 · 23 · H
Charnel
Hobarrow Bay · Purbeck Marine Wildlife Reserve ☆ V

5
LULWORTH RANGE WALKS
Legend, instructions & Warnings
see page 50
G · Kimmeridge Bay
Broad Bench

78

English Channel

6

77

88 · A · 89 · B · ³90 · C · 91

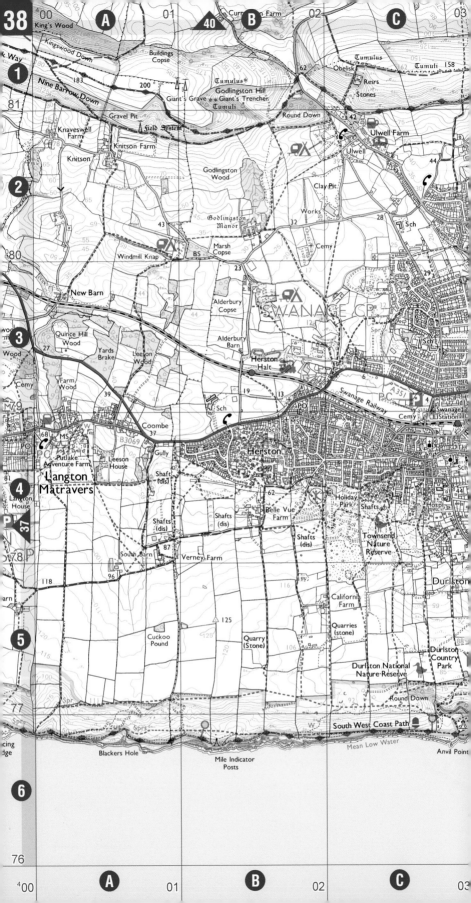

Glebeland Estate
71 04
E
41 05
F
06

1

Stone Seat
Ballard Down 117
BS
Purbeck
Way
Studland Hill
BSs
Tumuli
Ballard Cliff
Ballard Point

81

Whitecliff Farm

South West Coast Path

2

FB
19

Groynes

New Swanage
PC

°80

Hotel

P

Swanage Bay

3

Groynes

SWANAGE

79

Pier

V

IRB & LB Sta
Peveril Point
Lookout Station
PC

4

78

Durlston
Bay

5

P V PC

Durlston Head
Castle
Durlston Head
Globe
Mile Indicator
Posts
V PC

77

Tilly Whim
Caves

E n g l i s h   C h a n n e l

6

SZ

76

D
04
E
⁴05
F
06

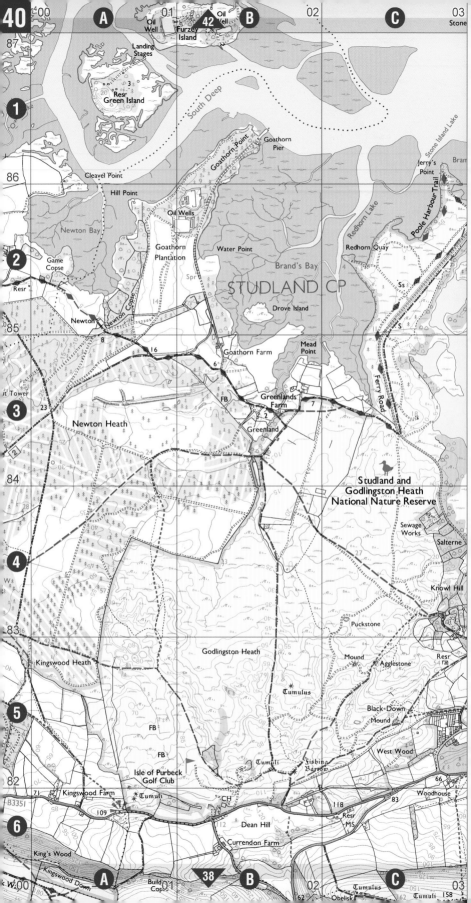

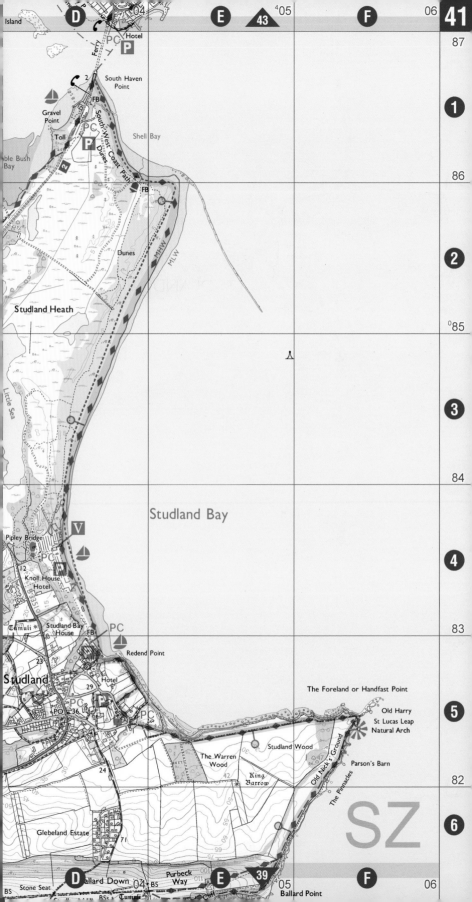

42

Pergins Island

A 00   B 01   C 02   03

1

92

Holes Bay

Creekmoor Lake

MHW

Upton Lake

2

Pontoons

91

POOLE

Longfleet

Sterte

Sch

Sch

Sch

Sch

Pol Sta

Stadium

Hosp

Hosp

Hosp

Poole Station

College

Coll

Offices

PC

Poole Park

P

PO

PC

Arts Centre

Boating Lake

3

90

Twin Sails Bridge

MHW

Back Water Channel

LB Sta

Pottery

Schs

Schl

Old Town

PC

Baiter

P

Poole Harbour Trail

Parkstone Bay

Marina

PC

Marina

Par

Lower Hamworthy

New Quay

Marina

Marina

Marina

4

FERRIES
CATAMARAN
St Helier
St Peter Port
SHIP
Cherbourg

Poole Harbour

Main

Ferry P (Summer)

89

UA Bdy

Wych Channel

5

Landing forbidden on North and shore between points A and

Shafts (dis)

Shafts

Cambridge Wood

Oxford Wood

West Lake

The Villa

Pottery Pier

Maryland

The Sanctuary

East Lake

88

Rough Brake

Fire Tower

Brownsea Island

St Michael's Mount

Harley Wood

Church Hill

Lincoln Cliff

Baden-Powell Outdoor Centre

Mon

24 W

Farm Buildings

Ramshorn Lake

William Pit

6

White Ground Lake

MHW

Harry Point

87

Slipway

Landing Stage

Oil Well

Oil Well

Furzey Island

Stone

00   A   Landing Stages   01   40   B   02   C   03

Upper Parkstone

Branksome

Branksome Park

Lower Parkstone

Parkstone

Sch

Cemy

Luscombe Valley

Compton Acres

Parkstone Golf Course

Lilliput

Marina

Groynes

Landing Stages

Canford Cliffs

Canford Cliffs

Canford Cliffs Chine

Channel

Pier

Poole Harbour Trail

Hosp

Flag Head Chine

Mud and Sand

PC
Poole Head

E9 European Long Distance Route 2

Poole Bay

East B

Brownsea Road

Groynes

Landing Stages

Pontoons

Landing Stages

Piers

Branksea Castle

North Haven Point

PC

Sandbanks

SZ

Ferry P (Summer)

Island

Hotel

HOW TO USE THIS INDEX

1. The map reference given refers to the actual square in which the feature is located and not the name.

2. A strict alphabetical order is used e.g. Blackers Hole follows Black Down but precedes Black Head

3. Names prefixed with 'The' are indexed under the main name, for example 'The Foreland' appears in the F section.

THE NATIONAL GRID REFERENCING SYSTEM

The grid lines form part of the National Grid and are at 1 km intervals.

To give a unique reference position of a point to within 100 metres proceed as follows:

Sample point: **Abbotsbury**

1. Read letters identifying 100,000 metre square in which the point lies (**SY**)

2. FIRST QUOTE EASTINGS - locate the first VERTICAL grid line to LEFT of the point and read the BLUE figures labelling the line in the top or bottom margin of the page (**57**). Estimate tenths from the grid line to the point (**7**). This gives a figure of **577**

3. THEN QUOTE NORTHINGS - locate the first HORIZONTAL grid line BELOW the point and read the BLUE figures labelling the line in the left or right margin of the page (**85**). Estimate tenths from the grid line to the point (**2**). This gives a figure of **852**

Sample Reference: **Abbotsbury SY 577 852**

South West Coast Path - Route Planner

Lyme Regis to Poole Harbour

Key: 🛈 Information Centre   🛏 Hotel / B&B   ▲ Youth Hostel   🍴 Restaurant   ☕ Cafe (Seasonal opening)   ⋀ Campsite (Seasonal opening)   🛒 Shop   🍺 Public House   ⛽ Petrol Station   〰 Ferry / Wade

From Lyme Regis

From Lyme Regis	From Poole Harbour	Location	Facilities
0 km	138.4	**LYME REGIS**	🛈 🛏 ⋀ 🍴 🍺 ☕ 🛒
		2km - Uplyme	🛏 ⋀ 🍴 🍺 ☕ 🛒 ⛽
4.9	133.5	**Charmouth**	🛏 ⋀ 🍴 🍺 ☕ 🛒
11.4	127	**Seatown**	🛏 ⋀ 🍴 🍺
		1km - Chideock	🛏 🍴 🍺 ☕ 🛒
14.5	123.9	**Eype Mouth**	🛏 ⋀ 🍴
16.3	122.1	**West Bay**	🛏 ⋀ 🍴 ☕ 🛒
		1.5km - Bridport	🛈 🛏 🍴 🍺 ☕ 🛒 ⛽
		0.5km - Burton Bradstock	🛏 ⋀ 🍴 🍺 ☕ 🛒 ⛽
		1.5km - Swyre	🛏 ⋀ 🍴 🍺 ☕
		2.5km - Puncknowle	🛏 ⋀ 🍴 🍺 ☕
25.3	113.1	**West Bexington**	🛏 🍴 🍺 ☕ 🛒
		4km - Litton Cheney	▲ 🛏
31.3	107.1	**Abbotsbury**	🛏 🍴 🍺 ☕ 🛒
		4km - Littlebredy	🛏
		2km - Portesham	🛏 ⋀ 🍴 ☕ ⛽
		0.5km - Fleet	🛏 ⋀ 🍴
		1km - Chickerell	🛏 ⋀ 🍴 🍺 🛒
48.8	89.6	**Weymouth**	🛏 ⋀ 🍴 🍺 ☕ 🛒 ⛽
		0.5km - Wyke Regis	🛏 ⋀ 🍴 🍺 ☕ 🛒 ⛽
52.3	86.1	**Fortuneswell**	🛏 ▲ 🍴 🍺 ☕ 🛒
		1km - Easton	🛏 🍴 🍺 ☕ 🛒 ⛽
57.8	80.6	Portland Bill	🛏 ⋀ 🍴 🍺 ☕ 🛒
75.5	68.6	**Weymouth**	🛏 ⋀ 🍴 🍺 ☕ 🛒 ⛽
		1km - Sutton Poyntz	🛏 🍴 🍺 🛒
		2.1km - Osmington	🛏 🍴 ☕
83.2	55.2	**Osmington Mills**	🛏 ⋀ 🍴 🍺
84.7	53.7	**Ringstead**	☕ 🛒
91.1	47.3	Durdle Door	⋀
93	45.4	**Lulworth Cove**	🛏 ▲ 🍴 🍺 ☕ 🛒
		2km - West Lulworth	🛏 🍴 🍺 🛒
104.5	33.9	Kimmeridge Bay	
		1.8km - Kimmeridge	🛏 ☕
		2km - Kingston	🛏 🍴 🍺
		4.5km - Corfe Castle	🛏 ⋀ 🍴 🍺 ☕ 🛒
		1km - Worth Matravers	🛏 ⋀ 🍴 🍺 ☕
114.1	24.3	St Aldhelm's Head	
		4km - Harman's Cross	🛏 ⋀ 🛒 ⛽
		2km - Langton Matravers	🛏 ⋀ 🍴 🍺 🛒 ⛽
123	15.4	Durlston Head	🍴 🍺 ☕
126.3	12.1	**Swanage**	🛈 🛏 ▲ ⋀ 🍴 🍺 ☕ 🛒 ⛽
		3km - Ulwell	⋀ 🍴 🍺

From Poole Harbour

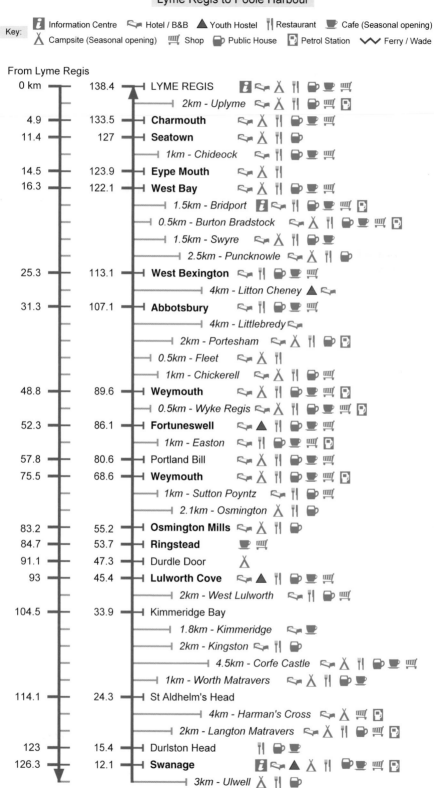

From Lyme Regis

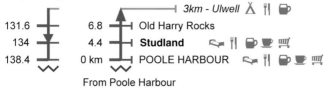

		3km - Ulwell
131.6	6.8	Old Harry Rocks
134	4.4	**Studland**
138.4	0 km	POOLE HARBOUR

From Poole Harbour

SOUTH DORSET RIDGEWAY ROUTE

Alternative shorter route between West Bexington and Osmington Mills

From West Bexington

0 km	26.9	**West Bexington**
		1km - Portesham
		1km - Upwey
		1km - Sutton Poyntz
24.8	2.1	**Osmington**
26.9	0 km	**Osmington Mills**

From Osmington Mills

- Most campsites and caravan sites are seasonal and may not be open in the winter, check before going.
- Some caravan sites are for Caravan Club members only, check before going.
- Some cafes and beach shops are only open in summer.

Ferry Information

Ferry	From	To	Reference	Frequency
Poole Harbour	**Studland** ∨∨ **Sandbanks**		1D **41** (SZ 036 868)	20 mins.

Operator: Bournemouth - Swanage Motor Road & Ferry Co.
Tel: 01929 450203
www.sandbanksferry.co.uk
All Year (07.00 - 23.00)

Tourist Information Centres

Name	Address	Telephone
Bridport	Town Hall, South Street, Bridport. DT6 3LF	01308 424901
Dorchester	11 Antelope Walk, Dorchester. DT1 1BE	01305 267992
Lyme Regis	Church Street, Lyme Regis. DT7 3BS	01297 442138
Poole	The Quay, Poole. BH15 1HJ	01202 253253
Swanage	The White House, Shore Road, Swanage. BH19 1LB	01929 422885
Wareham	The Library, South Street, Wareham. BH20 4LR	01929 552740

Danger Areas

LULWORTH RANGES - Pages 32 to 34.
On the south coast, between Weymouth and Poole.
The SW Coast Path runs through Lulworth Ranges.
There are also a number of circular walks within the Ranges and car parking facilities at Whiteway and Tyneham. Picnic facilities are also available at Whiteway car park.
Worbarrow Beach is open to the public when the Ranges are open.

For further information on live firing times, contact 01929 404819.

LULWORTH RANGE WALKS

LEGEND

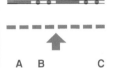

Road open when range walks open
(Ref. SY881801 to SY895815)

Range Walks

Range Walk starting point

A B   C
Beaches marked A, F, B to C,
D to E and G to H are open to the public when the range walks are open.

GENERAL INSTRUCTIONS

1. You must comply with the instructions of the wardens at all times.
2. You should not pick up any objects found on the range.
3. It is regretted that camping or fires are not allowed.
4. Please do not enter any building.
5. Please protect the wildlife. Do not collect specimens of flowers, birds, eggs, insects or fossils without permission.
   For safety's sake please do not leave the paths and do not touch any ammunition you may see.

WARNING

All visitors to Lulworth Ranges must take heed that this is an Army Range and the public have no right of access when firing is taking place. Visitors must keep within the Way Marks on each path. If people stray away from the clearly visible path Way Marks they can endanger themselves and others because only the designated paths have been cleared of explosive. Paths are marked on both sides by plain wooden posts with yellow bands. They are placed at about 50 to 100 metre intervals and are clearly visible. In addition the boundaries of the coast path from Gold Down to Worbarrow Bay and from Flower's Barrow to Arish Mell to Bindon Hill are marked by a fence and yellow tipped posts.
DO NOT CROSS THESE FENCES.

Wyke Regis Training Area & Chickerell Camp - Pages 21 and 22.
On the south coast, near Weymouth.
The SW Coastal Path runs along the northern boundary of Wyke Regis Bridging Camp and the southern boundary of Chickerell Range.
Access is available using Fleet Lane alongside Chickerell Camp following the Camp fence line to Chickerell Rifle Range, on Tidmoor Point on FP33, or Coastal Path FP36. Access is available at all times, except when red flags are flying when walkers will be diverted inland around the back of the Range firing point, by signs and access restricting gates, before returning to the Coastal Path.

For further information on live firing times, contact 01305 831935.

Safety & Security when walking

General

◆ Make sure you are wearing appropriate clothing and footwear, with suitable extra clothing in case the weather changes, or if you get delayed or misjudge how long it will take you to complete the walk.

◆ Be careful, if you are inexperienced, not to undertake a walk that is too ambitious.

◆ Take plenty to eat and drink, there are not always opportunities to buy extra provisions.

◆ Be sure someone knows where you are going and when to expect you back. Let them know when you have returned as well.

◆ Although taking a mobile phone is a good idea, in some remote areas there may not be a signal and therefore should not be relied upon.

◆ When walking on roads follow the advice in the Highway Code.

◆ Always use a pavement and safe crossing points whenever possible.

◆ Where there is no pavement it is better to walk on the right hand side of the road, facing oncoming traffic.

◆ Only cross railway lines at designated places and never walk along railway lines.

◆ Good navigational skills and a compass are essential.

◆ Always take warm and waterproof clothing; conditions at coastal locations can always change quickly, even in summer.

◆ Walking boots should always be worn.

◆ Gloves and headgear are advisable too in cold weather.

◆ Other essentials to take are; a waterproof backpack, "high energy" foods, a whistle, a torch (with spare batteries and bulb), a watch, a first aid kit, water purification tablets and a survival bag.

◆ Ready made first aid kits are available with all necessary items included.

◆ High factor sunscreen should be used in sunny weather, the sun can be particularly strong and can be hidden by sea breezes. Sunglasses are advisable too.

◆ Informal paths leading to beaches can be dangerous and are best avoided.

◆ When crossing a beach, make sure you know the tide times to avoid being cut off.

◆ Some cliffs overhang or are unstable and these are not always obvious.

◆ On the coast, mist, fog and high winds are more likely and can be hazardous.

> The international distress signal is six blasts of a whistle repeated at one minute intervals (the reply is three) or six flashes of light at one minute intervals (again the reply is three). In an emergency dial 999 or 112.

The Countryside Code

◆ Be safe - plan ahead and follow any signs.
Even when going out locally, it's best to get the latest information about where and when you can go; for example, your rights to go onto some areas of open land may be restricted while work is carried out, for safety reasons or during breeding seasons. Follow advice and local signs, and be prepared for the unexpected.

◆ Leave gates and property as you find them.
Please respect the working life of the countryside, as our actions can affect people's livelihoods, our heritage, and the safety and welfare of animals and ourselves.

◆ Protect plants and animals, and take your litter home.
We have a responsibility to protect our countryside now and for future generations, so make sure you don't harm animals, birds, plants, or trees. Fires can be as devastating to wildlife and habitats as they are to people and property.

◆ Keep dogs under close control.
The countryside is a great place to exercise dogs, but it's every owner's duty to make sure their dog is not a danger or nuisance to farm animals, wildlife or other people.

◆ Consider other people.
Showing consideration and respect for other people makes the countryside a pleasant environment for everyone - at home, at work and at leisure.

Useful Information

 Tide Times

Information on Tide Times
www.tidetimes.org.uk
includes sunrise and sunset times

Weather

Met Office
www.metoffice.gov.uk

 Countryside Access

For more information visit
www.naturalengland.org.uk

OS Map Reading

OS Map reading made easy

 OS National Grid

OS Using the National Grid

Danger Areas

Ministry of Defence Safety and Access
www.access.mod.uk

 Traveline South West

SW Public Transport Information
www.travelinesw.com
Getting from A to B by public transport

UKcampsite

Comprehensive campsite directory
for campers and caravanners
www.ukcampsite.co.uk